Health And Wholeness
Through The Holy Communion

JOSEPH PRINCE

Health And Wholeness Through The Holy Communion

ISBN 981-05-5184-3
© Copyright Joseph Prince, 2006

Joseph Prince Resources
www.josephprince.com

Printed in the Republic of Singapore
Fourth edition, twenty-sixth print: May 2016

contents

Introduction

As a young Christian growing up in a traditional church, what struck me most about the Holy Communion was God's judgment. I believed that unless I confessed all my sins before partaking, I would bring damnation upon myself.

At first, I tried to confess every single sin to get right with God before partaking, but after some time, I decided that it was easier to just not have Communion.

I believe that many Christians still have that same fear. And the average believer would have many unanswered questions and all kinds of worries about bringing judgment on himself. These stem from a misinterpretation of key verses on the subject.

Some Christians wonder if they can partake when they are not water baptised, while others are unsure if they need to attend classes before they can take the bread and wine.

When I became a pastor and had to minister the Holy Communion, my search for those answers led me to see the loving heart of

God expressed in the Lord's Supper. I discovered that God ordained the Holy Communion not as a ritual to be observed, but as a blessing to be received — the blessing of health and wholeness.

When you hold the bread in your hand, you are coming in touch with the greatest expression of His love. This love made Him endure the cruel stripes on His back and caused Him to subject His body to be beaten, bruised and broken so that yours can be whole. And when you partake, you celebrate and release your faith to receive His health and wholeness in exchange for your sicknesses and diseases.

When you drink the wine, you are reminded that the blood of the sinless Son of God did not just bring you forgiveness — it made you forever righteous, holy and blameless. So today, you have perfect standing before the Father and His ears are attentive to your softest sigh.

My prayer is that this book will help remove all your fears every time you approach His Table, and stir up your faith to receive the blessings of health and wholeness through His body and blood.

1

The Holy Communion — God's Channel Of Divine Health

chapter 1

The Holy Communion — God's Channel Of Divine Health

Next to being saved from hell or eternal destruction, divine health is the greatest blessing we can have.

Some people might say, "No, Pastor Prince. It would be great if I had lots of money. Then, I can do so many things." Well, I know of people who have lots of money. They have fleets of cars, but are not able to drive a single one of them because they are flat on their backs, sick.

> Jesus did not walk on water all the time, He did not calm storms all the time, but He healed all the time.

If someone is on his deathbed, I do not think he would say, "I wish I had made one more million." I believe he would be thinking, "If only I could have my health back. There are so many things to do, so many people to say 'I love you' to."

You can also have a great family with wonderful children, but if you are sick, and cannot run around and play with your kids, that would be sheer misery.

That is why I believe that health is the greatest blessing we can have while we are still here on earth. Without it, there is no way we can enjoy the blessings of God.

God's Nature Is To Heal

You will find that when Jesus walked on earth, most of His miracles were in the area of healing. That is because His nature is to heal.

The Bible says that Jesus *"… went about doing good and healing all who were oppressed by the devil, for God was with Him."* (Acts 10:38) He did not walk on water all the time, He did not calm storms all the time, but He healed all the time.

When God brought the children of Israel out of Egypt to bring them into the Promised Land, He made sure that none of them were sick.

> Psalm 105:37
> [37]**He also brought them out with silver and gold, and there was none feeble among His tribes.**

In Cecil De Mille's production of *The Ten Commandments*, a blind old man shuffled out of Egypt with a walking stick. That is how Hollywood dramatises the Holy Word. But it is incorrect.

God's Word says that there were none feeble, so that old man could not have been blind or bent over. Bible scholars estimate that there were about 2.5 million Israelites who left Egypt healed, healthy and whole. That was and still is God's will for His people today — all healed, healthy and whole.

Partaking Of The Lord's Body Brings Healing

If it is God's nature to heal, have you wondered why many Christians are sick? I am not referring to minor ailments like a cough or cold, I am referring to serious, life-threatening illnesses.

Now, if the people of the world are sick, it should not surprise us. They do not have Jesus Christ as their protection, so it is no wonder that they are sick.

But when believers are sick, I want to know why. And I do not want to draw my conclusions from human experience. I want an answer from God's Word.

You might be surprised to know that the Bible gives one and only one reason Christians are weak and sick, and die prematurely.

The apostle Paul, in 1 Corinthians 11:29–30, said, *"For he who eats and drinks in an unworthy manner eats and drinks judgment to himself, not discerning the Lord's body. For this reason many are weak and sick among you, and many sleep.*" Sleep here means death, not bodily rest.

Paul said, "*For **this** reason…*" He did not say, "for **these** reasons". He was pointing us to one singular reason Christians become weak and sick, and die before their time.

And what is "*this reason*" that Paul was highlighting to us? He said, "*… not discerning the Lord's body. For this reason…*" So the reason the Corinthians became weak and sick was their failure to discern the Lord's body.

> If we discern the Lord's body, we will walk in His health and wholeness.

It means that they did not know why they were partaking of the body when they came to the Table. They had no idea why they were eating the bread. And this was the reason they were not receiving the divine life of their Saviour, causing them to be weak and sick, and to die prematurely.

Since truth is parallel, it means that if we

do discern the Lord's body, we will walk in His health and wholeness.

This is only logical. Even my daughter will tell you that. When she was four years old, she came home from school one day and said, "Daddy, the opposite of tall is short. What is the opposite of small?" I said, "Big." "Good!" she said.

So it follows that if Paul said, *"... not discerning the Lord's body. For this reason many are weak and sick among you, and many sleep"*, then it must be that when we do discern the Lord's body, we will be strong and healthy, and live long.

You would have thought that Christians would study this passage so that they can walk in divine health. After all, Paul had singled out this one reason as the cause of sickness and, ultimately, premature death for many Christians.

Yet, it seems that most people in the body of Christ choose to focus on food and exercise as the key to living a healthy life. In fact, one of the best-selling themes in Christian bookstores today is food. There are all kinds of books on what to eat and what not to eat.

I am not knocking these books. What I am saying is that God does not want us to focus on food or exercise as the key to divine health. He does not want us to put our trust in natural means to stay healthy. 2 Corinthians 10:4 says, *"For the weapons of our warfare are not carnal…"*

Some people think that they will walk in divine health if they are on a Mediterranean diet since that was Jesus' diet. But let me remind you that the majority of the people whom Jesus healed were on a Mediterranean diet. They never had pork or prawns or any of that high-cholesterol stuff. Yet, they were still sick because natural solutions can only go so far.

By all means eat well and exercise. I watch what I eat and I hate oily stuff. I also exercise. But my trust is not in my own feeble human efforts. My trust is in God to keep me healthy. And God has ordained the Holy Communion as a key channel of health and wholeness for His people.

The early church believed this. That is why *"… they continued steadfastly in the apostles' doctrine and fellowship, in the breaking of bread, and in prayers."* (Acts 2:42) They majored on the majors. They made a big deal of those things that God made a big deal of.

They took God at His Word. It is no wonder that they experienced God's power. In Acts 2:43, 46, we read that they broke bread from house to house, and many signs and wonders were done through the apostles.

Although the body of Christ today understands the importance of doctrine, fellowship and prayer, few in the church truly understand the significance of the breaking of bread (or the Holy Communion). That is why many are weak and sick, and die before their time.

Down through history, powerful doctrines like "justification by faith" have come under severe attack by the devil. This is what has happened to the Holy Communion. The devil has pushed the church to two erroneous and extreme interpretations of this truth. On one side are the believers of transubstantiation* and, on the other, are people who have reduced the Holy Communion to a mere ritual.

---

*Transubstantiation is the alleged process whereby the bread and wine offered up at Communion are changed to that of the real body and blood of Jesus Christ.

Discern The Lord's Body Before Partaking

I believe that God wants to restore the true meaning and power of the Holy Communion to the church so that His people will rightly discern His body when they come to the Table. This will cause them to become strong and healthy, and to live long.

> The Holy Communion will add years to our lives and life to our years.

The Lord has made special provision for our health and this is all found in the death of His Son, the Lord Jesus Christ, when we come to partake at His Table.

It is one of my great passions in life to see the body of Christ receive every single thing that our Saviour suffered and died to give us. And I know that when God's people are correctly taught about how healing is dispensed at the Lord's Table, health and wholeness will follow. It will add years to our lives and life to our years.

After I released my message tape, *Health And Wholeness Through The Holy Communion*,

I received many testimonies of healing through the Lord's Supper.

I have a friend, Pastor Barnabas Mam, who is a pastor of pastors in Cambodia. God saved him from many life-threatening situations when the Khmer Rouge were slaughtering their own countrymen in the 1970s.

However, due to the impoverished state of things at that time, he developed some chronic physical conditions, including low blood sugar and calcium levels, insomnia and rheumatoid arthritis.

It was such a cruel irony that God's man of faith and power, who has a ministry accompanied by signs and wonders, had difficulty sleeping every night. He had to take sedatives and tranquillisers. And they did not always work.

His grandchildren also had to massage his swollen joints, which were racked with pain from the arthritis. His knees would give the most trouble, especially after more than two hours of preaching on his feet.

One morning, desperate after yet another sleepless night, his wife pulled out my tape on *Health And Wholeness Through The Holy Communion*.

He listened to it and faith just grew in his heart. He immediately prepared the elements and partook. That night, he slept like a baby!

The next morning, which was a Sunday, he stood up in church and shared on the power of the Lord's body to bring health when we come to His Table. After hours of being on his feet, he did not need a massage because he had been totally healed of chronic rheumatoid arthritis!

Till today, his wife is amazed at his healing. She says that she has found a new husband. He has new strength and can sleep at night.

Two weeks after he preached that message in church, he was sponsored to go for a full-body checkup in Malaysia. There, they found that his calcium and sugar levels were normal. Shortly after, he went for another checkup at a hospital in Phnom Penh and they too gave him a glowing report.

Around that time, a lady who was on his staff was healed of a longstanding migraine after she partook of the Lord's Supper. And this pastor friend of mine has since been receiving testimonies from people healed of all kinds of debilitating conditions after having Holy Communion.

When we recognise that the Holy Communion is God's channel of health and wholeness for His people, and we teach the church to rightly discern the Lord's body when they come to His Table, God's people will be healthy and strong, and will live long.

How To Discern The Lord's Body

chapter 2

How To Discern The Lord's Body

Having established that the Holy Communion is God's channel of health and wholeness for His people, it is time to find out how to experience that divine life that comes through discerning the Lord's body.

Notice that Paul said that it was not a failure to discern the blood, but a failure to discern the body that caused the people to be weak and sick, and to die before their time.

1 Corinthians 11:29–30

^{29}For he who eats and drinks in an unworthy manner eats and drinks judgment to himself, not discerning the Lord's body. ^{30}For this reason many are weak and sick among you, and many sleep.

Yet, when I was growing up as a Christian, I was taught that the two elements of the Communion should be lumped together. So I used to believe that the body and blood were both for the forgiveness of my sins.

God has since shown me that the body and blood should not be treated as one. There are two elements because there is a two-fold application in the Communion. The wine, which is His blood, is for our forgiveness. And the bread, which is His body, is for our healing.

The Blood Is For Forgiveness

The Corinthians, like most Christians today, had no problems discerning the blood. Paul's epistles make it very clear that the blood of

Jesus brings forgiveness of sins.

> Colossians 1:14
> [14]in whom we have redemption through His blood, the forgiveness of sins.

> Ephesians 1:7
> [7]In Him we have redemption through His blood, the forgiveness of sins, according to the riches of His grace…

Because the Son of God paid the penalty for your sins with His spotless blood, you can go scot-free when you put your trust in His blood to save you. When you partake of the wine, know that you are forgiven and have been made righteous. The blood of Jesus has given you right standing before God, so that you can come boldly into His presence. And when you pray, you can be sure He hears you.

The Bread Is For Healing

That is how you discern the blood and most

> When He spoke to the Syro-Phoenician woman regarding her daughter's healing, He called healing "the children's bread".

Christians understand that. But not many know how to discern the Lord's body.

To do that, we must first know what the bread represents. Jesus established that the bread, which is His body, is for our healing. How do we know that? When He spoke to the Syro-Phoenician woman regarding her daughter's healing, He called healing *"the children's bread"*.

Mark 7:26–28

[26]The woman was a Greek, a Syro-Phoenician by birth, and she kept asking Him to cast the demon out of her daughter. [27]But Jesus said to her, "Let the children be filled first, for it is not good to take the children's bread and throw it to the little dogs." [28]And she answered and said to Him, "Yes, Lord, yet even the little dogs under the table eat from the children's crumbs."

Notice that when she asked Jesus to cast the demon out of her daughter, He said that it was not good to give the *"children's bread"* to the *"little dogs"*. What does "bread" refer to? It refers to the healing that she was asking for. And what do "dogs" refer to? They refer to non-Jews or Gentiles like herself.

So Jesus was actually saying that healing was only for God's covenant people and not for Gentiles who were not included in the covenant then.

Having explained what Jesus meant, I should also go on to explain why I refer to bread as healing and not deliverance. Well, that is because the Bible treats disease and demon possession as the same thing since they both originate from the devil.

Acts 10:38 says that Jesus went about doing good and *"… healing all who were oppressed by the devil"*. Notice that disease is due to the devil's oppression. Thus, disease and demon possession are both the results of oppression by the devil and we need God's healing for these problems.

From this incident, it becomes clear that Jesus sees healing as the children's bread. The woman put her faith in that little crumb, and that act released power to drive the devil out of her daughter.

So the bread, even a small crumb, which is His body, is for our healing since we are now God's children and fully entitled to the healing bread.

What It Means To Discern The Body

In fact, I believe that when Jesus said, *"Take, eat; this is My body"* (Matthew 26:26), the disciples did not need any explanation like the one I just gave.

They knew that He wanted to impart to them His life, health and wholeness. These men were with Him every day and not once did they see Him sick. Not once did they see Him come down with a flu, fever or stomachache. He never had to say to them, "Can one of you preach the Sermon on the Mount for me? I don't feel up to it today." The Lord was never sick.

More than that, He was vibrant, full of life and full of health. When those who were without hands and feet were brought to Him, they were made perfectly whole. The body parts they needed were imparted to them from the heavenly store when they touched Him.

> Jesus' body was so filled with life that even His clothes were soaked with His health.

And His body was so filled with life that even His clothes were soaked with His health. The Bible says that a woman with an issue of blood for 12 years came to Him knowing that He was her only hope. (Mark 5:25–34)

She had spent all her money and suffered many things from many physicians. And what was the result? She was no better, but instead, became worse! Yet, with just one touch of the hem of His garment, she was immediately healed of the affliction.

If the hem of His garment could be soaked with His health, can you imagine His body?

No wonder Luke said, *"And the whole multitude sought to touch Him, for power went out from Him and healed them all."* (Luke 6:19) When a doctor, and Luke was a doctor, says this, you know that it is for real.

There was no need to tell the disciples that when He said, *"Take, eat; this is My body"*, He was imparting His life, health and wholeness to their bodies. They knew better than anyone else that taking the bread meant ingesting His health into their mortal bodies.

The Matzah Is An Object Lesson Of What Jesus' Body Symbolises

The matzah (a flat bread eaten during the Passover) is a good object lesson of what Jesus' body symbolises. The Mishnah or Jewish oral laws gave instructions on the preparation of this bread. These instructions should be of great interest to us.

According to these laws, the bread was to be unleavened, baked, pierced with holes and striped. Till today, the Jewish rabbis do not know why the bread has to be prepared this way. But blessed are your eyes for they see the grace of God.

No leaven was used because leaven in the Bible represents sin, and Jesus is the perfect, sinless Son of God. That is why He is able to take our sins upon Himself.

His body was burnt because the full fury of God's wrath against our sins fell on Him. This fire was supposed to fall on us and our families, but it fell on Jesus instead.

His side was pierced and He bore those merciless stripes on His back so that our bodies might be made whole.

So when you come to the Lord's Table, make sure that you discern His body. When you partake, believe that Jesus took bread and broke it because His body was going to be broken.

> As you partake of His broken body, know that His body was broken so that yours can be whole.

And as you partake of His broken body, know that His body was broken so that yours can be whole. When you partake in this spirit of faith, something happens to your body. You become strong, healthy and you will live long.

The Lord's Supper Brings The Double Cure

By now, it should be clear that the blood and the body have two different applications. This is consistent throughout the Bible.

The prophet Isaiah said, *"Surely He has borne our **griefs** and carried our **sorrows**…"* (Isaiah 53:4, NKJV) The Young's Literal Translation or YLT Bible provides a more accurate translation for the words "griefs" and "sorrows", stating that *"Surely our **sicknesses** He hath borne, and our **pains** — He hath carried them…"*

Similarly, in the Gospel of Matthew, this verse was interpreted as *"He Himself took our **infirmities** and bore our **sicknesses"**.* (Matthew 8:17)

In the Greek, "infirmities" or *astheneia* means bodily weaknesses. So we can see very clearly that Isaiah was saying that the Messiah would take upon His own body, our bodily weaknesses, sicknesses and pains. In other words, Jesus bore **not just our sins**, but also **our bodily weaknesses, sicknesses and pains**. This is what some hymn writers of old called the "double cure".

This double cure is evident in the Passover. The Lord's Supper was first celebrated on the same day as the Passover because it is the true Passover.

> Luke 22:15–20
> [15]Then He said to them, "With fervent desire I have desired to eat this Passover with you before I suffer; [16]for I say to you, I will no longer eat of it until it is fulfilled in the kingdom of God." [17]Then He took the cup, and gave thanks, and said, "Take this and divide it among yourselves; [18]for I say to you, I will not drink of the fruit of the vine until the kingdom of God comes." [19]And He took bread, gave thanks and broke it, and gave it to them, saying, "This is My body which is given for you; do this in remembrance of Me." [20]Likewise He also took the cup after supper, saying, "This cup is the new covenant in My blood, which is shed for you.

The Old Testament is the shadow, the New Testament is the real substance. Jesus is the true, perfect, unblemished, holy Lamb of God. So the Passover is a type of the Lord's Supper.

During the first Passover, they killed the lamb and put the blood on the doorposts. This caused the destroyer to pass over their families because God said, *"And when I see the blood, I will pass over you; and the plague shall not be on you to destroy you..."* (Exodus 12:13)

The blood was for the people's forgiveness. The blood covered the people's sins and appeased the righteous requirements of God.

But what did they do inside the house?

Exodus 12:8

[8]Then they shall eat the flesh on that night; roasted in fire, with unleavened bread and with bitter herbs they shall eat it.

If the body of a "shadow lamb" could bring such supernatural results, how much more the body of the true "substance lamb", our Lord Jesus Christ!

They ate the roasted lamb and the unleavened bread. This was to give them strength for the journey. It was not natural strength that they received. It was supernatural.

That is why there were *"… none feeble"*. (Psalm 105:37) It takes a supernatural work of God for 2.5 million people to all be healthy.

We know that this lamb was a mere shadow of the real substance. So if the body of a "shadow lamb" could bring such supernatural results, how much more the body of the true "substance lamb", our Lord Jesus Christ!

Here, again, the double cure was at work — the blood was for forgiveness, and the body and bread were for divine strength. No wonder when they left Egypt, there were none feeble.

David described the double cure this way, *"Bless the Lord, O my soul, and forget not all His benefits: who forgives all your iniquities, who heals all your diseases"*. (Psalm 103:2–3) Notice that His benefits include the forgiveness of our sins as well as the healing of our diseases.

> Healing, like forgiveness, is not a promise. It is the blood-bought right of Christians!

When Jesus took our punishment on the cross, it did not just bring us forgiveness, it also brought us healing.

Most people, when asked whether they are sure of their forgiveness, say they are. They know that God has already forgiven them because of the cross. But when asked if they are sure of their healing, they say they are not.

I want you to know that at the cross, Jesus bore our sins and our sicknesses. And so healing, like forgiveness, is not a promise. It is the blood-bought right of Christians!

Because of what He did at the cross, we do not just have forgiveness, we also have healing. Forgiveness and healing go hand in hand. The faith that you have for forgiveness is the same faith that will bring your healing.

A Testimony Of Healing Through The Holy Communion

When you believe and when you rightly discern the Lord's body, you will experience miraculous healings and wholeness when you partake of the Holy Communion.

One church member, Albert, experienced this in a spectacular way. Some time in November

2002, Albert was told by doctors that his mother had a 3cm cancerous growth in the rectum. There was little cause for worry as the removal of such tumours is usually fairly straightforward.

A few days before the operation, two leaders of the church visited her at the hospital and shared the gospel with her. She was born again that day and Albert was very happy that things were really working out well. The operation proceeded without complications and she was discharged within days.

Months later, she was re-admitted for a scheduled follow-up surgery to close the stoma (an opening created in the previous operation). Complications arose at this stage, resulting in her having to undergo three more operations.

By the fifth surgery, this dear 75-year-old lady was drained of all energy and her body started to react negatively. Both her temperature and pulse rate shot up, and her lungs became filled with water.

Her condition deteriorated to the point where the surgeon felt that it was necessary to inform the family to prepare for the worst. He told them that in cases like this, there is a very strong likelihood that the patient would not pull through, and made it clear that the next three days would be crucial. If she did not improve within that time, it was unlikely that she would survive.

Albert was thrown into a state of shock and confusion. He felt helpless. He did not know what to do. But he knew that God would not let his mother undergo five operations and still allow her to die. He was sure that God is not like that. He had always known God to be faithful.

He felt desperate and lost but had a strong urge to have Holy Communion with his mother and family. So he got his sister and father together, and told them that they should partake of the Lord's Supper because that would bring resurrection life to his mother.

His family members were baffled. They did not understand how he could believe that some wine and bread would bring health and wholeness to someone so critically ill. He simply made no sense to them.

But Albert had been listening to my tape on *Health And Wholeness Through The Holy Communion* over and over again. He knew that when we partake of the Lord's body, there would be an infusion of His incorruptible life into our bodies.

He had also been reading the four Gospels, and found that all four writers, Matthew, Mark, Luke and John, had included the Lord's Supper in their accounts. He was sure that if Jesus saw it fit to tell us something four times, that truth must be very powerful.

Though unconvinced, his father, sister and brother-in-law agreed to do as he said. He prepared the bread and wine, and the entire family went into the intensive care unit (ICU).

It was cold and everyone was silent. It felt very strange to have Communion in a place like that. He did not know what to do and just started praying in tongues.

After that, he declared that by Jesus' stripes and His broken body, his mother is healed. He stepped forward and placed a small crumb in his mother's mouth and poured some of the grape juice in. He felt a sweet and strong presence of God in the room, and he somehow knew that his mother had been healed. He left the room with peace in his heart.

But nothing happened. One day passed, then another. On the morning of the third day, he made his way to the hospital as usual and headed for the cafeteria to have breakfast. There, he received a call from the nurse. In an urgent tone, she said, "Albert, something has happened to your mother. You'd better come now."

He did not know what to expect. But the thought that ran through his mind was, "She cannot be dead. I know she cannot be dead."

He rushed to the ICU, pushed open the door and dashed to his mother's bedside. He leaned forward to look at her, and when he saw that she was conscious, he sank to his knees and wept. He lifted his voice and praised the Lord. All that he had hoped for, prayed for and believed God for had finally happened.

After this, his mother started getting better and within a week, all the tubes were removed and she was eating again.

Today, she has regained at least 15kg and is up and about, helping her daughter bake cookies, and calling up relatives and friends to tell them about Jesus! Doctors feared that she would not make it. But the resurrection life of Jesus filled her body when her family partook of the Lord's Supper with her.

Healing Through The Holy Communion Can Also Be Gradual

Although this precious 75-year-old lady experienced a spectacular miracle, healing through the Holy Communion can also be a gradual process. As you partake, you will get better over time. The more you partake, the better you get.

I personally experienced this. Years ago, I had a skin condition that troubled me. I went to the doctor and he said that it could be cured, but the medicine would have side effects. I said, "Thank you very much," and left.

God's healing is so much better. There are no side effects. So I partook of the Lord's Supper and claimed by faith the full benefits of His broken body for me in this area. Yet, nothing seemed to happen at first.

After some time, I stopped bringing this matter before God, but I continued partaking in faith. Then one day, I realised that I was totally healed. I cannot tell when exactly that condition left, but I know that as I continued to partake, I simply got better. The drama was not there. It was not spectacular. But it was still supernatural!

The Power Of Proclaiming The Lord's Death

One other lesser known aspect of the Holy Communion is the power of proclaiming the Lord's death. Paul said, *"For as often as you eat this bread and drink this cup, you proclaim the Lord's death till He comes."* (1 Corinthians 11:26)

You might ask, "Pastor Prince, what about the Lord's death are we proclaiming and to whom are we proclaiming it?" Paul said in another place, *"Having disarmed principalities and powers, He made a public spectacle of them, triumphing over them in it."* (Colossians 2:15)

So when we remember Jesus' death, we are also proclaiming to the principalities and powers that they have been disarmed because He has triumphed over them.

Some years back, a couple from our church

owned a house which most people would call "haunted". It is more accurate to say that there were demons hanging around that place. This is not uncommon because demons usually congregate in places where tragic incidents like fatal accidents and murders have taken place.

One of the tenants felt spooked because his family complained that they saw "a figure moving around in the house". Two of my associate pastors and a deacon went over to that house, and took the Lord's Supper there. When you have Holy Communion, you are proclaiming to demon spirits that Jesus reigns.

And when you release your faith in the finished, complete and perfect work of Jesus at the cross, every knee must bow and every tongue confess that Jesus is Lord. This means that every demon has to flee. So just by proclaiming the power of the Lord's death, that house was cleansed of demons.

From that time on, there were no more complaints. The couple now have a new tenant and have had no more problems in this area.

You Don't Need A Pastor To Partake

Jesus told us to have Communion often. So there must be something powerful about it. Do you think that He would make us do something often without having our blessing in mind?

Those who believe in the power of that one perfect sacrifice on the cross know that His blessings of health, wholeness and preservation abound at His Table.

> Have the Holy Communion as often as you need to.

Once you are a believer, you are a priest. (1 Peter 2:9) So you can partake of the Lord's Supper and even minister it to others. You do not need a pastor to do it.

In the church, we pastors do it because we are the spiritual authority over the people, and there must be order in how we conduct things.

But outside the church, you, as a royal priest, are qualified to partake on your own. Do as Jesus said — have it often. "How often?" you might ask. As often as you need to. It depends on how much you want His health and wholeness.

I am not saying that you must partake every day. But if you are sick, I would recommend that you have Communion daily.

I know of people who are so radical that they take it like medicine — three times a day. And you know what? They get radical results.

Some people say, "Pastor Prince, don't be extreme." Those of us who trust in God and in His Son's perfect work at Calvary are extreme — extremely blessed. So partake because the Holy Communion is God's channel of health and wholeness for you.

Don't Be Afraid To Partake

chapter 3
Don't Be Afraid To Partake

God has made it truly easy for His people to walk in divine health. We just need to come to His Table, put our faith in His broken body for our healing and partake. It is so simple, yet so powerful.

That is why the devil has tried to steal this truth from the church by making Christians believe that they should not partake. And he does this by making them believe that they are unworthy to come to the Lord's Table. This erroneous thinking is largely due to a misinterpretation of the following verses.

> 1 Corinthians 11:29–30
> [29]For he who eats and drinks in an unworthy manner eats and drinks judgement to himself, not discerning the Lord's body. [30]For this reason many are weak and sick among you, and many sleep.

When I was a young Christian, I was told, "Don't come to the Lord's Table if you have sin in your life. If you are unworthy and partake, you are guilty of the body and blood, and will drink judgment to yourself."

I was not sure what all that meant, but it was enough to scare me. And I was always told, "Be sure to examine yourself to see if you have sin in your life. And make sure you confess all your sins before you come."

I never dared to partake because I always wondered, "Is there some sin that I have not confessed?" It is not that I was living in sin, but I did not want to take the risk.

What if I forget to confess one sin? Judgment would fall on me, right? And my mama sure didn't raise no fool. So I chose not to partake, just to be safe. Every time the elements of the Communion were passed to me, I just passed them on.

I thought that I was better off not partaking. But ironically, by not coming to the Lord's Table, I was robbing myself of God's source of health, healing and blessing for me. Legalistic and erroneous teaching is very damaging because it keeps us from receiving what God has for us.

What It Means To Partake Unworthily

So let us read for ourselves what Paul said so that we can partake in a worthy manner.

1 Corinthians 11:27–29, KJV

[27]Wherefore whosoever shall eat this bread, and drink this cup of the Lord, unworthily, shall be guilty of the body and blood of the Lord. [28]But let a man examine himself, and so let him eat of that bread, and drink of that cup. [29]For he that eateth and drinketh

unworthily, eateth and drinketh damnation to himself, not discerning the Lord's body.

Firstly, in verse 29, he says that if you eat and drink unworthily, you bring damnation to yourself. Let us get one thing straight. The word "unworthily" is an adverb, which means it modifies the verb.

In this case, "unworthily" describes the action of eating and drinking. It is not describing the person who is eating or drinking. So Paul was not saying that if you are an unworthy person, do not partake.

Yet, the church has somehow misconstrued that teaching and now, Christians are saying, "If you are unworthy, don't partake." They say, "If you have sin in your life, don't come to the Lord's Table lest you become weak and sick, and die prematurely." They have turned something that is meant to be a blessing into a curse.

In any case, all of us who come to the Lord's Table are unworthy and made worthy only by His blood. It is only Jesus' death that qualifies us to partake. Paul was not saying that we should not partake if we are unworthy. He was saying that we should not partake in an unworthy **manner**.

What does it mean to partake unworthily? Read the rest of verse 29 and you will conclude that if you fail to discern or understand the significance of the Lord's body, you are eating and drinking in an unworthy manner.

> Partaking unworthily means not recognising that the broken body of the Lord was meant to bring health and wholeness.

The Corinthians partook unworthily because they did not recognise that the broken body of the Lord was meant to bring them health and wholeness.

And by treating the Holy Communion as a ritual, they missed out on the blessings. They did not understand the significance of the bread. They did not know why they were partaking. This is what it means to partake unworthily.

The manner in which we partake will determine whether we experience the benefits of the Lord's body. If our attitude is, "It's just a piece of bread," then that is what it will be. And we will have robbed ourselves of the life-giving effects of the bread at His Table.

Paul described in greater detail the manner in which the Corinthians partook. Let us take a closer look.

1 Corinthians 11:20–22

²⁰Therefore when you come together in one place, it is not to eat the Lord's Supper. ²¹For in eating, each one takes his own supper ahead of others; and one is hungry and another is drunk. ²²What! Do you not have houses to eat and drink in?…

He gave them a good tongue-lashing because when they came to the Lord's Table, those who were hungry rushed for their turn. And others guzzled the wine until they became drunk.

So Paul was not saying that if you have sin in your life, you cannot partake*. He was telling us to partake in the correct manner, which is to recognise that the Lord's body was broken so that

*Please do not misunderstand me. I am against sin, but this is not the point of Paul's teaching here.

ours can be made whole. Do not take the Lord's Supper because you are hungry. If you are hungry, eat at home first.

What Paul told the Corinthians to do was to discern the power of the Lord's broken body. He was teaching us that when we fail to discern the body, we should not partake because we are not claiming by faith what Jesus has done for us.

And by failing to do so, we are making His work on the cross ineffective and powerless as far as we are concerned.

When you fail to discern His body, you are actually despising His work on the cross. Vine's Expository Dictionary has this to say about partaking unworthily:

> Unworthily — *anaxios* NT: 371 is used in 1 Corinthians 11:27, of partaking of the Lord's Supper "unworthily", i.e., treating it as a common meal, the bread and cup as common things, not apprehending their solemn symbolic import.

Jesus wants us to take the bread and believe that His body was broken so that our bodies can be made well. And when we discern it that way, we are partaking worthily.

When you come to His Table and release your faith in the Lord's body, you will receive the benefits of healing, health and wholeness. And you will be strong and healthy, and live long.

What It Means To Examine Yourself

Secondly, I was told that to "examine" myself means to check if I have sins in my life and to confess them all.

To correct this misconception, we have to understand the context of Paul's statement. He is addressing the issue of eating and drinking unworthily.

So it follows that he was telling the Corinthians that they should examine themselves to see if they were eating and drinking in a worthy manner. Nowhere does it say that he told them to examine themselves to see if there was sin in their lives.

1 Corinthians 11:27–29

[27]Therefore whoever eats this bread or

drinks this cup of the Lord in an unworthy manner will be guilty of the body and blood of the Lord. [28]But let a man examine himself, and so let him eat of the bread and drink of the cup. [29]For he who eats and drinks in an unworthy manner eats and drinks judgment to himself, not discerning the Lord's body.

Looking at the passage again, it is clear that Paul is saying that a man should examine himself to see if he is eating and drinking worthily so as not to eat and drink judgment to himself.

It is so simple, but preachers have for so long made Christians fearful and sin-conscious when God wants us to be Son-conscious. He just wants us to examine ourselves to see if we are putting our faith in His Son's work on the cross for us.

What It Means To Drink Judgment To Yourself

Thirdly, the "judgment" (in verse 29) does not mean God's anger or wrath as I used to think. In some circles, people still believe that

> The Lord's Supper is how God helps us offset the process of ageing and walk in divine health.

the judgment here refers to God sending them to hell. That is an incorrect interpretation.

The Greek word used here is *krima*, which means divine sentence. When Adam sinned against God, a divine sentence fell on the human race. Weakness, sickness and death are some effects of that divine sentence.

As long as we are here on earth, our bodies are subject to the ageing process, which is part of the divine sentence. All our bodies are decaying every day. Our brain cells are dying daily.

The Holy Communion is God's solution for us to offset the decay. And even your friends will see the results. They will begin to ask you, "Hey, why do you seem to look younger and younger? You never seem to age!"

One day, when we get to heaven, we will have brand new bodies that never grow old, never tire and never look bad. Meanwhile, the Lord's Supper is how God helps us offset this process of ageing and walk in divine health. Every time you partake, you are reversing the effects of the curse or divine judgment in your body.

The Devil Is No Match For Those Who Believe In The Power Of The Lord's Broken Body

I believe that for a long time, the devil has tried to blind the church to the power of the Lord's body. And that is because he knows that he is no match for those who have faith in the power of Jesus' broken body.

Let me give you an example of how a church member faced a spiritual attack but overcame it through the Lord's Supper.

In late 2003, my church organised many trips to Israel. Each tour group consisted of 120 people. In all, we had 1,500 people visiting the Holy Land. On one of the trips, a lady in her twenties, Suwen, developed deep vein thrombosis during the flight to Israel.

This is a rare condition that results from a clot in a deeply situated vein in the thigh or leg. It is called the "economy class syndrome" because some people develop this condition when the seats are cramped and the humidity level is low. A clot will form which, if it makes its way to the lung, can cause respiratory failure. And when that happens, it can result in death.

Suwen felt a pain in her right calf during the flight. As she was disembarking from the plane, she suddenly collapsed. Her eyes rolled up and she started foaming at the mouth. The airline personnel were extremely professional and immediately called for an ambulance to take her to the hospital.

On the way to the hospital, her heart suddenly stopped. The clot had travelled from her leg to her heart and finally to one of her lungs, causing a cardiac arrest. When the ambulance reached Assaf Harofeh Medical Center, she had already turned blue. They wheeled her to the accidents and emergency ward where they tried to resuscitate her.

The doctors asked for her next of kin because they believed that she was not going to survive. They were about to pronounce her dead, but miraculously, after a last-ditch attempt, they managed to revive her heart.

However, she was in a critical condition as the clot made breathing difficult. She was unconscious and there were all types of tubes running through her nose and throat. Doctors were monitoring her closely, fearing that the clot might bring about respiratory failure.

That very evening, her husband, sister and brother-in-law, who are all firm believers in the power of the Lord's body to bring healing, partook of the Lord's Supper together, speaking health and wholeness to her body.

I was with my leaders in another part of Israel at that time and could only get to where she was four days later. When we arrived at the hospital, doctors informed the family that her condition had worsened. My leaders and I partook of the Holy Communion, and pronounced the benefits of the Lord's broken body upon Suwen.

The very next day, she regained consciousness and the doctors who were keeping a close watch on the clot could no longer find it! They did not know what to think and dared not be too optimistic.

They kept her under close observation, but day after day, though they looked for the clot, they were unable to find it. At the same time, she started getting stronger. After a week, they discharged her.

Once she left the hospital, she joined the next tour group and visited the Garden Tomb, where the resurrection of the Lord took place.

Her family members shared after the whole episode that they initially felt fearful and lost. However, due to the teaching they had been receiving, they knew that this was not the work of God, but an attack of the devil.

They were extremely encouraged when they remembered the testimony of Albert's mother who was healed when she took the bread and wine in the ICU. So they were very confident that by partaking of the Lord's Supper, health and wholeness would come upon Suwen.

There Is Power In the Act Of Eating

In the midst of intense spiritual attack, we will experience victory when we believe that what Jesus did on the cross is greater than any attack of the devil. And once we realise how much Jesus suffered so that our bodies can be made whole, we will be confident that partaking of His broken body will bring healing to our bodies.

If you still find it hard to believe that eating a small crumb can bring your body health and wholeness, let me point you back to the Garden of Eden. There, Adam merely ate a fruit and he plunged the whole human race into sin. His sin was what brought disease and, ultimately, death.

So God in His mercy and wisdom devised a perfect solution. Since the **simple act of eating** by Adam brought disease and death, He ordained that the **simple act of partaking** of a crumb would bring health and wholeness to His people.

Partaking Of The Holy Communion

Let us now partake of the Lord's Supper and release faith for our forgiveness and healing.

Before you partake, just know that God wants you to *"prosper in all things and be in health, just as your soul prospers"*. (3 John 1:2)

Prepare the bread and wine, and do not be in a rush. Remember, this is not a ritual. You are about to personally experience afresh His love for you.

Hear Him say to you, " Take, eat. This is My body, which is broken for **you**." See His eyes burning with love as He says to you, "This cup is the new covenant in My blood, which is shed for **you**."

See the Lord carrying all your sins and diseases. He took your sins in His body on the cross. See Him taking on His body your physical conditions too. If you have a tumour, see the tumour on His body. Whatever disease you might have, see it on His body. It is no longer on you. See His health come on you.

Surely He bore your sins and carried your diseases. So as you partake, release your faith in the bread and the wine.

Hold the bread in your hand and say this:

> **Thank You Jesus for Your broken body. It is for my healing, my spouse's healing and my children's healing. Thank You that by Your stripes, by the beatings You bore, by the lashes which fell on Your back, we are completely healed. I believe and I receive. (Eat the bread.)**

Next, take the cup in your hand and say this:

Thank You Jesus for the new covenant cut in Your blood. Your blood has brought me forgiveness and washed me from every sin. I thank You that Your blood has made me righteous. And as I drink, I celebrate and partake of the inheritance of the righteous, which is preservation, healing, wholeness and prosperity. (Drink the wine.)

Thank You Jesus, I love You because You first loved me.

Testimonies

Testimonies of miraculous healings through the Lord's Supper continue to pour in. Some of them are recorded here for your encouragement.

Polyp Supernaturally Expelled After Taking Holy Communion

Since July 2003, I experienced spotting (light, sporadic bleeding) after my menses was over. It would continue for six to seven days.

Sensing that something was wrong, I consulted my gynaecologist. Various physical examinations and ultrasound scans were done, but nothing was detected. Finally, he could only attribute the bleeding to a hormonal imbalance. I was worried when the doctors could not help me.

Sometime in mid December, after Pastor Prince did a fresh round of teaching on the importance of the Holy Communion, my husband, our two girls and I started taking the Lord's Supper as a family on a daily basis.

On 23 February 2004, while standing at the dinner table and scooping some food for my daughter, I passed out a lump about 2.5cm in size. I was a little surprised and exclaimed to my husband that this must be a miracle.

The following day, I brought the lump to the hospital to let the doctors run tests to determine its nature and content. The report showed that the polyp was not cancerous (see histopathology report).

Since then, the spotting has totally stopped and I praise God that because of His miracle, I was spared a painful procedure where the gynaecologist would have had to scrape the polyp off the walls of my uterus.

Praise Jesus — He bore my sins and sicknesses on the cross and as I partake of His finished work through the Holy Communion, I am healed. Needless to say, our family continues to celebrate the Lord's Supper daily. To God be all the glory.

Stephanie Wong

Histopathology Report

TO:
NATIONAL UNIVERSITY HOSPITAL
REF NUMBER: 20040552001D
DEPARTMENT: GYNAECOLOGY
CONSULTANT: SINGH KULDIP
SOURCE: CLG
PROJECT: CHARGEABLE

ACCESSION NO: 2004-NB-002504

NAME: WONG MARY STEPHANIE
NRIC:
SEX: Female
DOB: AGE:
RACE:

DATE RECD: 25/02/2004
PATHOLOGIST 1: G C RAJU (A/PROF)
PATHOLOGIST 2: CHAN JOEY PUI-JEUNG (DR)

DATE OF RPT: 27/02/2004

Histopathology Report

SPECIMEN RECEIVED

Nature of specimen not indicated on label.

GROSS DESCRIPTION

Polypoid mass measuring 2 x 1.5 x 0.8 cm. Entire specimen processed in one block.

MICROSCOPIC DESCRIPTION

Polyp shows proliferative endometrial glands and fibrotic stroma with thick-walled blood vessels.

There is no evidence of malignancy.

DIAGNOSIS

Mass passed per vaginum - Benign endometrial polyp

Healed Of Menstrual Cramps

All my life, I suffered from menstrual cramps until God healed me when I took the Holy Communion.

Some months ago, when it was that time of the month again, I was hit by a really bad wave of pain. My hands and feet were cold and clammy, and my face was as white as a sheet. I lay on the bed, rolling from side to side and groaning in pain.

Being a new believer, I did not know very much about what Jesus had done on the cross for me. Thankfully, I was with my fiancé at that time, and he is a "believing believer". He rushed to the kitchen to get some grape juice and bread, and we had Communion. Miraculously and instantly, the pain ceased.

His mother explained to me that Jesus carried our pains and diseases on the cross, and that included menstrual cramps. At that time, I did not know what she meant.

But now, I do. As I attended church for the whole of last year, I realised that surely, not maybe, He has borne our sicknesses and pains.

My faith came by hearing and hearing the Word of Christ.

After that incident where I was healed through the Holy Communion, whenever the pain came during my menses, I would say, "Pain, go in Jesus' name because He has taken my pain on the cross." Then, I would have Communion. I thank Jesus that it has been a year since I last experienced cramps.

Recently, I met up with some old friends and they shared that they were taking pills and avoiding cold drinks to ease the pain of menstrual cramps. I now know that there is an easier way — believing that Jesus' work on the cross also provided healing for us.

He died to take our pains because He wants our joy to be full. I realised that His heart must have ached when He saw me in pain in the past. How can you be joyful when you are clutching your stomach in pain?

Today, I even take cold drinks when I am having my menses and I no longer experience any pain. Praise Jesus! What He has done in my life does not stop here. There is so much that He has given me and done for me. He has really transformed me over the years and has brought me so much joy. He is so amazing. I could go on and on about His wonders in my life.

Adelind Yeo

Sixteen-Month-Old Baby Healed Of Acute Liver Failure

My 16-month-old daughter, Joy, had been having fever and a runny nose for about a week. During that time, I brought her to the general practitioner several times, but the medication given did not help.

When her condition grew worse and she started throwing up, we brought her to the hospital and they warded her immediately. The doctor's initial diagnosis was that she had gastric flu and a chest infection. This was later changed to acute liver failure.

To our bewilderment, we were told that her liver was failing so rapidly that she only had a 20 per cent chance of survival. A liver transplant was recommended but even with that, her chances of survival were upped by only another 30 per cent.

The news came as a shock to us. Only a week ago, everything was rosy. Now, I felt like my whole world had crumbled. The thought of losing my daughter made everything that had been important before seem trivial. My concerns about not being at work became irrelevant. Guilt and regret swept over me as I thought of the happy times we had as a family and how limited they were due to our many commitments.

In the midst of all that turmoil, I decided to call up a friend from New Creation Church to ask for prayer even though I was not a Christian then. He got one of his pastors to come over to pray for us.

That day, 5 March 2004, Pastor Mark led me in the salvation prayer. He and his assistant, Christina, then prayed for Joy. After that, we had Holy Communion and they proclaimed that because Jesus' body was broken, little Joy's would be made whole.

Hope swelled in my heart for the first time that day and I felt a comforting warmth enfolding me. A vision of me carrying Joy in church flashed across my mind and a fleeting thought hit me

— Joy would be healed and we would proclaim this testimony to the world. I did not dare share this with anyone, not even my husband. I did not want to get their hopes up too high. Yet, I now felt like I could cast my cares on God.

But the sight of my little baby with needles and tubes of all sizes sticking out from every part of her frail body was heartrending. I could not bear to watch as the nurses groped for fresh veins to insert their needles into. They even had to resort to the veins in her armpits and opened up a little hole near her stomach area to introduce a tube.

In the past, all I could do was stand around helpless, but this time, I was able to pray. And I discovered that prayer was not difficult. It was a natural heartfelt cry to my heavenly Father.

Initially, I begged God to return Joy to me. I told Him to take my life instead of hers. I was desperate for a miracle, but did not really know how to pray. Thank God that He did not answer that prayer.

Instead, He sent Christina to teach me how to pray. From her, I came to see that God loves my girl much more than I did. I realised that I did not have to give up anything for her healing because Jesus gave up His very life to purchase this healing for her.

Christina told me to claim this benefit of healing from His perfect work on the cross. She told me that every negative report about Joy was only temporary. But what Jesus has done is permanent.

I began to speak Psalm 91 over Joy and even boldly thanked God for all the plans He had in store for her. I was most encouraged when a colleague of mine, also from New Creation Church, came and declared a verse from Psalm 118 over Joy, *"You shall not die, but live, and declare the works of the Lord."*

On Saturday, Joy's condition worsened and she turned yellow due to jaundice. Doctors explained that her liver was deteriorating to the point where only a transplant could save her. My husband, sister and I had volunteered to be donors. We were told to go home to get some rest that evening as they needed to run tests on us for the transplant the next day.

But the rest that we had hoped for never came because our older daughter Victoria, who was two and a half years old then, began displaying the same symptoms that Joy had. She woke up at three in the morning with a fever and was vomiting. I prayed but decided to send her to the hospital for a checkup.

At about 6.45am on Sunday, after the doctor had confirmed that Victoria was all right, he showed me Joy's latest laboratory report. This very caring and well-meaning doctor took me through page after page of bad news, and told me that a transplant was necessary to save Joy.

But as he was going on, I rejected every negative report silently in my heart. I remembered Christina's words that these were but temporary, and that my girl was already healed.

I had been having Communion daily and claiming His healing for Joy. In fact, I had staked out a little corner in the hospital where our friends and family would gather to worship and pray. I must have caused quite a commotion, but the hospital staff were gracious at all times.

Some of them were concerned that I might be so hyped up by all the prayer that when the bad news came, I would not be able to face up to reality. One person was even heard saying,

"She prays so much, does she actually think that there's going to be a miracle?"

But I didn't care. I just kept looking to Jesus. I asked Him to send us the best doctors, nurses and helpers. I even prayed that every drop of medication would be administered by God Himself. I asked the angels to watch over her and thanked God that every minute, He was reconstructing her liver and giving her a brand new organ.

At about 10.30am that same morning, the doctor suddenly showed up at the ward looking very grim. I braced myself for the worst. My heart was again ready to refute every negative report. But instead of bad news, he said that Joy's liver was rejuvenating. He said that at the rate she was improving, she might not need a transplant. My entire family were beside themselves with joy.

After the long mental and emotional struggle, I suddenly found this piece of news too good to be true. I wondered if they were just saying that to make me feel better. I questioned if it was wise to become too hopeful at this point. After all, it was only four hours ago that I was reading those gloomy reports. I called Christina.

She could not stop rejoicing and I began to thank God as the impact of His work slowly sank into my heart.

Strengthened, I made my way to church for the 2pm service. The presence of God in that place was unbelievable. The moment I stepped in, I felt God's love wash over me. I just cried tears of gratitude and joy.

When I reached the hospital after the service, the doctor came with more updates. We were told that Joy was "too well to be on the transplant list"! Later, the kind doctor told me that Joy was very "lucky" because they did not do anything special that could have caused such a recovery. I knew it was not luck, and just continued praising and thanking God for the miracle!

On Monday, the day of the scheduled transplant, instead of more surgical procedures, ironically, we witnessed needle after needle and tube after tube being removed from our little girl. And within days, she was transferred out of the intensive care unit (ICU).

By Wednesday, relatives of many of the other patients in the paediatric ICU ward approached me to ask how the miracle happened. I just shared with them how God, in His love, healed my daughter and asked Pastor Mark to pray for their loved ones. So he just went around the ward praying for the sick.

In less than two weeks, my little bundle of joy was discharged. All glory to Jesus for He truly put the joy back into all our lives!

Samantha Wong

Healing Of The Sole

I had been experiencing a sharp pain in the sole of my right foot after straining it during a workout. Initially, I left it alone thinking that it would go away. Six months later, my sole was still hurting.

In fact, it worsened to the point where it affected my walking and even standing. It caused considerable pain whenever I stepped on the pedal while playing the keyboard during our Mandarin service. To make matters worse, I sprained my right knee during aerobics.

I prayed over my foot and claimed healing, but nothing happened. I even tried foot reflexology to ease the pain, but this was only temporary. The pain would return a few hours after.

Some time in February, a friend bought my husband and me some matzah from Israel. In March, we started taking the Holy Communion on a daily basis every morning before going to work. Within two weeks, the pain in my sole left. My sprained knee was also completely healed.

I cannot pin down the exact day or date the healing took place. I realised it one day when I put my full weight on my right foot and found that there was no more pain. When it dawned on me that a miracle had happened, I jumped around just to test out my healing. My sole and knee felt as good as new.

I must confess that how healing comes through the Holy Communion is beyond my understanding. But I do not need to know everything before I start doing what the Lord has said is good for me.

I cannot imagine what my husband and I must have missed out on by not taking the Lord's Supper. Now that He has shown us a glimpse of how His body gives us divine health and His blood brings us divine righteousness, we will continue to partake and rest in His finished work.

Katherine Soh

Salvation Prayer

If you would like to receive all that Jesus has done for you, and make Him your Lord and Saviour, please pray this prayer:

Lord Jesus, thank You for loving me and dying for me on the cross. Your precious blood washes me clean of every sin. You are my Lord and my Savior, now and forever. I believe that You rose from the dead and that You are alive today. Because of Your finished work, I am now a beloved child of God and heaven is my home. Thank You for giving me eternal life, and filling my heart with Your peace and joy. Amen.